D0455695

# The Bathroom Trivia Book

By Jack Kreismer

RED-LETTER PRESS, INC.
SADDLE RIVER, NEW JERSEY

# The Bathroom Trivia Book

## NUGGETS OF KNOWLEDGE FOR AMERICA'S FAVORITE READING ROOM

The Bathroom Library™

**THE BATHROOM TRIVIA BOOK**
**Revised & Updated 1995**
**Copyright © 1986 Red-Letter Press, Inc.**
**ISBN: 0-940462-03-6**
**All Rights Reserved**
**Printed in the United States of America**
For information address Red-Letter Press, Inc.
P.O. Box 393, Saddle River, N.J. 07458

*"A bathroom reader is like royalty. They both occupy the throne for endless periods of time."*

—*j.k.*

# The
# Bathroom
# Trivia Book

Thomas Paine, the author of *Common Sense* and the creator of the name "United States of America", died in obscurity June 8, 1809. Only six people came to his funeral in New York.

• • • • • •

## Bathroom Trivia

When Joseph Gayetty invented toilet paper in 1857, he had his name printed on each sheet.

• • • • • •

The average caterpillar has sixteen legs.

• • • • • •

Before 1814 U.S. Congressional Representatives were paid six dollars per diem. And that was only when Congress was in session.

• • • • • •

How many times can a woodpecker peck? Twenty times a second.

• • • • • •

When the Shell Oil Company first opened its doors, it was a seashell novelty shop.

## Trivia Test

What King became President of the United States?

*Leslie King. When his parents divorced, he was adopted by his stepfather and given a new name, Gerald Ford.*

Laugh and you'll burn up three and a half calories.  No joke.

•  •  •  •  •  •

A man's outhouse has the sun on the door, while the "ladies' room" has a crescent.

•  •  •  •  •  •

Rats can't vomit.

•  •  •  •  •  •

There are 293 ways to make change for a dollar.

•  •  •  •  •  •

When asked to name a color, three out of five people will say "red".

•  •  •  •  •  •

Talk is cheap compared to what it once was.  In 1915, a telephone call from New York to San Francisco cost $20.70 for the first three minutes.

•  •  •  •  •  •

At 90 degrees (F) below zero your breath will freeze in midair and fall to the ground.

•  •  •  •  •  •

Credit Fritz Lang for the familiar countdown, "three, two, one, liftoff". The phase appeared in his 1929 film *Die Frair im Mond* (*The Woman in the Moon*).

•  •  •  •  •  •

The Delicious apple was originally known as the Hawkeye.

•  •  •  •  •  •

Most people take an average of seven minutes to fall asleep.

• • • • • •

England's Queen Anne (1665-1714) outlived all of her seventeen children.

• • • • • •

"Pif, paf, pof" is the Dutch answer to the "Snap, crackle, pop" of Rice Krispies.

• • • • • •

The tallest man in the world was 8'11" Robert Wadlow. He was just 22 years old when he died in 1949 from an infection caused by leg braces he needed to keep him on his feet.

• • • • • •

Ohio is listed as the 17th state in the U.S., but technically it is number 47. Until August 7, 1953 Congress forgot to vote on a resolution to admit Ohio to the Union.

• • • • • •

A squirrel lives about nine years.

• • • • • •

In 1885 the Home Insurance Company of Chicago was the tallest building in the world. The skyscraper was nine stories tall.

## Bathroom Trivia

In ancient Rome, it was commonplace for a woman's bath to have a tub filled with donkey milk and spiced with perfumed swan's fat.

• • • • • •

The female praying mantis devours her male partner while mating.

• • • • • •

A fly's taste buds are in its feet.

• • • • • •

"Wanted: Young, skinny, wiry fellows not over 18. Must be expert riders, willing to risk death daily. Orphans preferred. Wages $25.00 a week." —If you fit this mid-1800's help wanted ad, you'd have been a perfect candidate for the Pony Express.

• • • • • •

Edwin "Buzz" Aldrin was the second man to walk on the lunar surface. His mother's maiden name was Moon.

• • • • • •

This one may be tough to swallow, but an alligator can supposedly wolf down an eight pound chicken in one gulp.

• • • • • •

The comic strip *Peanuts* was originally called *Li'l Folks.*

• • • • • •

In 1944, Fidel Castro was voted Cuba's best schoolboy athlete. A left-handed pitcher, Castro was later given a tryout by the Washington Senators but was turned down by the baseball club.

• • • • • •

Peach Melba was named after Australian opera star Nellie Melba (1861-1931) who was the first to be served the dessert by its creator, a French chef named Escoffier.

• • • • • •

Official studies have found that right-handed people tend to scratch with their left hand and vice-versa.

• • • • • •

Rock 'n'roller Chuck Berry has a degree in cosmetology from Gibbs Beauty College.

• • • • • •

A cat has a normal body temperature of 101.5. A dog's is 101.

• • • • • •

Bees flap their wings 300 times a second.

• • • • • •

No U.S. president has been an only child.

• • • • • •

Reykjavik, Iceland is warmer than Chicago, Illinois in the winter.

• • • • • •

John Wayne had an 18 inch neck.

• • • • • •

## Bathroom Trivia

According to an old Massachusetts law, you're not allowed to shave while driving a car.

• • • • • •

Rubber bands last longer when refrigerated.

• • • • • •

A parrot's vocabulary is generally no more than twenty words.

• • • • • •

## Trivia Test

Gary Dahl introduced a new breed to America in the 1970's. What was it?

*The Pet Rock.*

---

An ostrich's intestinal tract is up to 45 feet long.

• • • • • •

The name of the dog featured on a box of Cracker Jacks is Bingo. The little sailor boy is, of course, Jack.

• • • • • •

Ernest Lawrence Thayer received five dollars for writing the poem *Casey at the Bat* in 1888.

• • • • • •

7'1" former basketball great Wilt Chamberlain is the son of 5'8" parents.

• • • • • •

A U.S. government-backed study found that pigs can become alcoholics.

• • • • • •

An eyelash lives about five months.

• • • • • •

The word *taxi* is spelled the same in English, German, French, Swedish and Portuguese.

• • • • • •

The Mulberry Garden was once a center of prostitution in London, England. It is now the site of Buckingham Palace.

• • • • • •

# By The Numbers

*It's time to do some serious bathroom thinking. Listed in the left hand column below are numerical trivialities. On the right are clues to their significance. See how many you know.*

| Trivia | Clue |
|---|---|
| 1. 24,896 miles | What on earth! |
| 2. 1,860 steps | Tall order |
| 3. 5 Exeter Place | "Hello" |
| 4. 31,622,400 seconds | Hop to it! |
| 5. 127 feet 3 3/8 inches | Roughly, a diamond |
| 6. 116 years | War games |
| 7. 225 squares | My word! |
| 8. 53310761 | "Hounddog" |
| 9. 1 Cherry Street | By George |
| 10. 59 minutes | Saved by the bell |

*Answers next page*

# Answers—By The Numbers

1.  *Circumference of the earth at the equator.*

2.  *Number of steps to the top of the Empire State Building.*

3.  *Boston address where the telephone was invented.*

4.  *Number of seconds in a leap year.*

5.  *Distance from home plate to second base on a baseball diamond.*

6.  *How long the 100 Years War lasted.*

7.  *Number of squares on a Scrabble board.*

8.  *Elvis Presley's military dog tag number.*

9.  *Washington's presidential address in New York.*

10. *The total amount of time from opening to closing bell in a 15 round boxing match.*

## Bathroom Trivia

Surveys have concluded that the average person will use the bathroom six times during the average workday.

• • • • • •

A cow's sweat glands are in its nose.

• • • • • •

The national anthem of Greece has 158 verses.

• • • • • •

The World Trade Center's twin towers in New York City have two zip codes, 10047 and 10048—one for each building.

• • • • • •

The U.S. Government will not allow portraits of living persons to appear on postage stamps.

• • • • • •

Mozart never went to school.

• • • • • •

Smokey the Bear's original name was *Hot Foot Teddy.*

• • • • • •

Queen Elizabeth was an eighteen year old mechanic in the English military.

• • • • • •

The watch pocket in pants is also known as the *fob.*

• • • • • •

The actual playing time in a big league baseball game which lasts two and a half hours has been clocked at 9 minutes and 55 seconds.

• • • • • •

In ancient China, doctors received their fees only if their patients were kept healthy. If their health failed, the doctor sometimes paid the patient.

●　●　●　●　●　●

140 members of the Lodi Diving School in California played a Monopoly marathon in 1976 for 1,008 consecutive hours—underwater.

●　●　●　●　●　●

German-sounding items were a no-no in the United States during World War I. Americans took to calling sauerkraut "liberty cabbage".

●　●　●　●　●　●

Six people can feast on one scrambled ostrich egg for breakfast.

●　●　●　●　●　●

We don't know if there's a Heaven on earth, but there is a Hell. It's a town in Norway.

●　●　●　●　●　●

The dot over the letter i is called a *tittle*.

●　●　●　●　●　●

Mormon leader Brigham Young invented the department store.

●　●　●　●　●　●

After Custer's Last Stand, Sioux Indian leader Chief Sitting Bull became an entertainer and toured the country with Buffalo Bill's Wild West Show.

●　●　●　●　●　●

Dixieland to Dixie Cups? Ice cream maker Tom Carvel started out as a Dixieland musician.

• • • • • •

Dirty snow melts faster than white snow because it's darker and absorbs more heat.

• • • • • •

Peanuts are one of the ingredients of dynamite.

• • • • • •

A telephone signal travels 100,000 miles a second.

• • • • • •

An elephant is not afraid of a mouse.

• • • • • •

Did you know that the square-topped cap worn at graduation ceremonies is a *mortarboard* ?

---

## Trivia Test

"La Giaconda" is the actual title of what famous piece of art?

*Mona Lisa.*

---

In 1949, the University of Southern California's Division of Fine Arts conducted a poll to select the man with "the most nearly perfect male figure". The winner—Ronald Reagan.

• • • • • •

## Bathroom Trivia

U.S. Patent 3,593,345 was granted for the "whisper seat", a toilet seat with soundproof lining to prevent noise from being heard by others.

• • • • • •

# The One and Only

The honey bee is the only bee that dies after stinging.

• • • • • •

The only person whose birthday is a legal holiday everywhere in the U.S. is George Washington.

• • • • • •

The only mammal that can fly is the bat.

• • • • • •

The only thing named from the U.S. Patent Office itself is "patent leather".

• • • • • •

James Buchanan was the only bachelor president.

• • • • • •

Maine is the only state in the U. S. which has only one syllable.

• • • • • •

Lake Michigan is the only one of the Great Lakes entirely in the U.S.

• • • • • •

The bee is the only insect that produces food which is eaten by man.

• • • • • •

Nepal is the only country which does not have a rectangular flag. It has two triangular pennants, one on top of the other.

* * * * * *

The only letter not used in the spelling of any of the 50 states in the U.S. is "q".

* * * * * *

The great horned owl is the only animal that will eat a skunk.

* * * * * *

Henry Wadsworth Longfellow is the only American to have a bust at Westminster Abbey in London.

* * * * * *

The kiwi is the only bird that has nostrils at the end of its bill.

* * * * * *

AT&T claims the average person makes 1,140 calls per year.

• • • • • •

Abraham Lincoln did not set foot in Illinois, "The Land of Lincoln", until he was an adult.

• • • • • •

The Japanese term *kamikaze* means "The Divine Wind".

• • • • • •

For some odd reason, the oak tree is struck more than any other by lightning.

• • • • • •

Three men who killed Sir Edmund Berry were hanged for the murder in 1911 at London's Greenberry Hill. Their last names were Green, Berry, and Hill.

• • • • • •

Astronauts on the moon weigh only one-sixth of what they do on earth.

• • • • • •

Jaguars are scared of dogs.

• • • • • •

You can preserve your unrefrigerated ground camel meat with garlic.

• • • • • •

The National Safety Council reports that the object most often choked on by Americans is the toothpick.

• • • • • •

Alan Alda was reportedly paid $150,000 per episode for his role as Hawkeye Pierce on the *M\*A\*S\*H* television sitcom.

• • • • • •

## Bathroom Trivia

Kleenex was called *Celluwipes* when first marketed in 1924.

• • • • • •

Franklin Delano Roosevelt originated the word *chiseler*.

• • • • • •

Just in case anyone asks you how many points there are on the leaf of the Canadian flag, you can answer, with certainty, 11.

• • • • • •

Montgomery Ward's first catalogue was printed in 1872—on one sheet of paper.

• • • • • •

Singer Ray Charles dropped his last name, Robinson, in order to avoid confusion with boxing great Sugar Ray Robinson (whose real name is Walker Smith).

• • • • • •

The words loosen and unloosen mean the same thing.

• • • • • •

Almost half the bones in your body are in your hands and feet.

• • • • • •

Istanbul, Turkey is in two continents—Europe and Asia.

• • • • • •

Toads do not have teeth.

• • • • • •

Dutch treat: Donald Duck is known as *Anders And* in the land of wooden shoes.

• • • • • •

There are more chickens than people in the world.

• • • • • •

## Bathroom Trivia

In colonial times, a plumber was called a *plumbum* worker.

• • • • • •

Plymouth Rock weighs seven tons.

• • • • • •

Eli Whitney didn't profit much from his cotton gin, but did make a lot of money as a gun manufacturer.

• • • • • •

The roller coaster was invented in Russia in the 17th century.

• • • • • •

Your brain is 80 percent water.

• • • • • •

MAFIA is an acronym for *Morte Alla Francia Italia Anela*—"Death to the French is Italy's Cry".

• • • • • •

An average pair of feet will sweat about one-half of a pint of perspiration a day.

• • • • • •

A peacock is a male. The female is called a peahen.

• • • • • •

The man who created Wonder Woman was William Moulton Marston. a psychologist who also invented the polygraph. Honest.

• • • • • •

Have you heard of the acronym H.O.M.E.S.? It is said to be the best way to remember the names of the five Great Lakes— Huron, Ontario, Michigan, Erie, and Superior.

• • • • • •

A flamingo can only eat when its head is upside down.

• • • • • •

In Japanese, there is no single word to say "yes" or "no".

• • • • • •

The only ten-letter word you can create using the top line of letters on a typewriter keyboard is *typewriter*.

• • • • • •

The Chinese celebrate birthdays only once every ten years.

• • • • • •

Abraham Lincoln died in a bed slept in by his assassin, John Wilkes Booth.

• • • • • •

# Footnotes

There are more sweat glands on the soles of your feet than any other part of your body.

• • • • • •

African elephants stay on their feet for 30 or 40 years. It's no wonder that they suffer from flat feet.

• • • • • •

After a decade of research, the Goodyear Rubber Company concluded that shoes wear out faster on the right feet than on the left feet.

• • • • • •

In just one day, an average person takes about 18,000 steps. And in an average lifetime, a person will walk the equivalent of almost three times around the world.

• • • • • •

It wasn't so tough to follow in the footsteps of George Washington. He wore a size 13. On the other hand, or foot, Robert E. Lee's shoe size was only 4 ½.

• • • • • •

The most popularly sold shoe in America is the tennis shoe with a 50% foothold on the market.

• • • • • •

A hummingbird can't stand on its own two feet. They're not strong enough to hold up the bird on a flat surface.

• • • • • •

Your feet swell through the day and can become as much as 5 to 10 percent bigger at the end of the day than they were in the morning.

• • • • • •

Shirley Temple was the original choice to play Dorothy in *The Wizard of Oz* but the child wonder's studio, 20th Century Fox, wanted too much money so MGM decided to go with Judy Garland.

• • • • • •

It is a misdemeanor to kill or threaten a butterfly—so says City Ordinance No. 352 in Pacific Grove, California.

• • • • • •

The cat's meow dept.—A survey claims the most popular name for a male cat is "Tiger"; for a female, it's "Samantha".

• • • • • •

The state flower of Alaska is, appropriately, the forget-me-not.

• • • • • •

Folding money, invented by the Chinese, was first made of deerskin.

• • • • • •

## Bathroom Trivia

England's Worcester Canoe Club set the world record for paddling a hand-propelled bathtub. The 25 man team covered a distance of 55 miles, 425 yards in 24 hours on September 28 and 29, 1979.

• • • • • •

Counting sheep dept.—There are ten times as many of them in Australia as there are people.

• • • • • •

Researchers have found that, on the left hand, the ring finger is longer than the index finger in only three out of ten women, but in six of ten men the ring finger wins hands down.

• • • • • •

After Wyatt Earp retired as marshal of Tombstone, Arizona he moved to San Francisco and became a boxing referee.

• • • • • •

The term *red tape,* meaning "bureaucratic delay", comes from the color of tape which was used to tie official papers in England as far back as the mid 1600's.

• • • • • •

Chewing gum magnate William Wrigley Jr. started his working career as a soap salesman.

• • • • • •

Ancient Egyptians shaved off their eyebrows to mourn the death of their cats.

• • • • • •

*Beetle Bailey* was banned from the comic pages of the U.S. military's newspaper *Stars and Stripes.*

• • • • • •

A hockey puck weighs .38 lb.

• • • • • •

A dog's heart beats 40 times a minute faster than yours does.

• • • • • •

The handshake is a friendly gesture today, but it originated in ancient times out of suspicion. Strangers shook hands to show that they were unarmed.

• • • • • •

# License To Brag

*Celebrity Car Plates*

| | |
|---|---|
| Alex Haley | KINTE |
| Jack LaLanne | REDUCE |
| Sally Struthers | TACKY |
| Robert Stack | UNTCHBL |
| Leslie Uggams | SMAGGU (Uggams in reverse) |
| Wayne Newton | VEGAS - 1 |
| Lawrence Welk | A1ANA2 |
| Flip Wilson | KILLER |
| Valerie Perrine | RATS ("star" backwards) |
| Ernest Borgnine | BORG 9 |
| Tim Conway | 11 YEARS (That's how long *The Carol Burnett Show* was on the air.) |
| Foster Brooks | A LUSH |

• • • • • •

In an average lifetime, the human body produces more than 25,000 quarts of saliva.

• • • • • •

The shortest distance from the east coast to the west coast in the U.S. as the crow flies is from Jacksonville, Florida to San Diego, California—2,092 miles.

• • • • • •

Tuna fish swim at an average speed of 9 miles per hour constantly. They never stop moving.

• • • • • •

Yankee Noodle Dandy: Thomas Jefferson introduced macaroni to the United States—and ice cream—and waffles.

• • • • • •

A Metropolitan Life Insurance study found that major league baseball players live significantly longer than the average male—especially third basemen.

• • • • • •

Alaska's coastline is longer than that of all the U.S. coastal states combined.

• • • • • •

Habit-forming government: The people of Dubuque City, Iowa elected Carolyn Farrell mayor in 1980—the first nun to become so honored in a U.S. town.

• • • • • •

A domestic cat has eighteen claws, five on both of the front paws and four each on the back paws.

• • • • • •

In an official test conducted by University of Missouri Professor Harold V. Biellier in 1978 and 1979, a white leghorn hen laid 371 eggs in 364 days, the highest amount on record.

• • • • • •

The superstition that "three on a match" is unlucky comes from the Boer War when British soldiers thought that lighting three cigarettes on one match would give the enemy time enough to aim and fire.

• • • • • •

Akron, Ohio is "The Rubber Capital of the World". It also boasts the world's largest fishing tackle industry.

• • • • • •

The tip of a whip makes a cracking noise because it moves faster than the speed of sound.

• • • • • •

An ear of corn almost always has an even number of rows. You're likely to find them in rows of twelve, fourteen or sixteen.

• • • • • •

Earthworms have five hearts.

---

### Trivia Test

Only two U.S. Presidents are buried in Arlington National Cemetery. One is John F. Kennedy. Who is the other?

*William Howard Taft*

---

Experts say that Julius Caesar's autograph is worth more than any in the world—two million dollars. Maybe that's because one hasn't been found yet.

• • • • • •

The only domestic animal not mentioned in the Bible is the cat.

• • • • • •

In the English language, more words begin with "s" than any other letter. In descending order, the top ten word starters are s,c,p,a,t,m,e,d,r and f.

• • • • • •

23 year old George Armstrong Custer was the youngest man ever to become a general in the U.S. Army.

• • • • • •

The average person swallows 295 times while eating a meal.

• • • • • •

The only U.S. president to hold a Ph.D. was Woodrow Wilson.

• • • • • •

Honking horns on wedding cars dates back to the old practice of blowing horns and ringing bells at newlyweds to ward off evil spirits.

• • • • • •

The left bank of a river is the left side as you look downstream.

• • • • • •

The Fisherman's Information Bureau in Chicago registers the catches of large and record-sized fish. The organization is known by its initials.

• • • • • •

Peter Minuit may have gotten a bargain when he bought New York from the Indians for $24 in 1626, but he got more than he bargained for twelve years later when he drowned after a terrible storm struck his crew on a trading expedition to the West Indies.

• • • • • •

In the 1800's in England, anyone who unsuccessfully attempted suicide faced the death penalty.

• • • • • •

*Circadian dysrhythmia* is another flighty term for jet lag.

• • • • • •

The heaviest snowfall ever recorded in the U.S. was in 1921 when 76 inches fell on the town of Silver Lake, Colorado.

• • • • • •

Buddy Ebsen was selected to be the Tin Man in *The Wizard of Oz*, but had to turn down the role when he suffered a collapsed lung from inhaling metal dust in the costume.

• • • • • •

The male mosquito does not bite—only the female does.

• • • • • •

## Bathroom Trivia

Among the items the U.S. Patent Office has in its files is a toilet lid lock (U.S. Patent 3,477,070) to prevent unauthorized access to the toilet.

• • • • • •

The most common surname in the world is "Chang".

• • • • • •

A golf ball, when driven off a tee, can reach speeds up to 170 miles per hour.

• • • • • •

Henry Hudson sailed the Hudson in 1609, but the river named for him had actually been discovered more than eighty years earlier by a Portuguese, Estavan Gomez.

• • • • • •

In 1911 a West Point applicant flunked his physical, so the military school granted admission to the next candidate—Dwight D. Eisenhower.

• • • • • •

A Chinese checkerboard has 121 holes.

• • • • • •

A secretary's left hand does 56 percent of the typing.

• • • • • •

Pluto, the Disney dog, was originally called Rover.

• • • • • •

*Dixie,* the popular Confederate song during the Civil War, was written by Dan Emmett, a Northerner.

• • • • • •

A female African elephant can be pregnant for almost two years.

• • • • • •

Martin Van Buren was the first U.S. born citizen to become president.

• • • • • •

One cord of wood can make seven and one-half million toothpicks.

• • • • • •

At this very moment, 70 percent of Americans driving on the highway are speeding.

• • • • • •

It takes eight minutes for light to travel from the sun to the earth.

• • • • • •

M&M's stands for the last names of Forrest Mars Sr., the candymaker, and his associate Bruce Murrie.

• • • • • •

The bride wears red in China.

• • • • • •

A cow can give 100 quarts of milk per week.

• • • • • •

It took Noah Webster twenty years to put together his first dictionary, *The American.*

• • • • • •

The only mobile U.S. National Monument is San Francisco's cable cars.

• • • • • •

There are three words in the English language with two u's in consecutive order—vacuum, residuum, and continuum.

• • • • • •

### Bathroom Trivia

Elvis Presley had a reading chair in his bathroom.

• • • • • •

Until 1936, it was against the law in New York to wear topless bathing suits—for both men and women.

• • • • • •

# If At First You Don't Succeed

In 1832, he was a 22 year old business failure. The same year he ran for the legislature and was defeated. In 1833, he was a business failure once more. In 1836, he was said to have suffered a nervous breakdown. In 1838, he lost in an effort to become Speaker of the House in the State Legislature. Five years later, he ran for Congress. Again it was in vain. In 1846, he ran for Congress and won, only to lose his re-election bid in 1848. He ran for the U.S. Senate in 1854 and lost. He ran for the Vice-Presidential nomination in 1856 and lost that, too. One more time he ran for a Senate seat, in 1858. He lost. In 1860, he became the sixteenth President of the United States.

The world's biggest clams weigh almost five hundred pounds.

● ● ● ● ● ●

Bathroom quote—"Bing sings like all people think they sing in the shower."—Dinah Shore, about crooner Bing Crosby.

● ● ● ● ● ●

East Chicago is a town in Indiana.

● ● ● ● ● ●

The strongest muscle in your body is in your tongue.

● ● ● ● ● ●

The odds against a mother having twins are 90 to 1.

● ● ● ● ● ●

Donkeys aren't the only jackasses. A variety of penguins are called jackasses too.

● ● ● ● ● ●

Thomas Jefferson cooked up the original recipe for chicken a la king.

● ● ● ● ● ●

There are three words in the English language in which one letter is repeated six times: *degenerescence* (six e's), *indivisibility* (six i's), and *nonannouncement* (six n's).

● ● ● ● ● ●

The eggplant was a "mad apple" and believed to be poisonous in the 1800's.

● ● ● ● ● ●

## Bathroom Trivia

Tribeca Communications published a 1984 book by Lana Toni Gersman titled *Dear John*. It is a guide devoted entirely to the best toilet seats in New York City.

• • • • • •

"Jack" is the most common name in nursery rhymes.

• • • • • •

An adult has 206 bones. A newborn infant has 300.

• • • • • •

Jim Thorpe won the pentathlon in the 1912 Olympics. The fifth place finisher was U.S. General George S. Patton.

• • • • • •

The first minimum wage was established in America in 1938. It was 25 cents per hour.

• • • • • •

More than 50 percent of the time spent in U.S. courtrooms involves automobile cases.

• • • • • •

It was George Washington who nicknamed New York the *Empire State*.

• • • • • •

The Tokyo Zoo in Japan is closed for two months a year to give the animals a vacation from the visitors.

• • • • • •

Alaska doesn't have any counties.

• • • • • •

# The Presidency—20 Questions

1.  What was Abraham Lincoln's middle name?

2.  Which two presidents died on July 4, 1826?

3.  Name the only president born on July 4.

4.  Where did President Harry Truman live in 1950?

5.  What was the name of the pony Caroline Kennedy used to ride on the grounds of the White House?

6.  What chief executive was an ex-president for 31 years, the longest time a former president lived following his term of office?

7.  Name the only man to be both president and vice-president yet never elected to either office.

8.  What was George Washington's salary as president?

9.  How long must one be a resident of the U.S. in order to become president?

10. Who was the widow of Colonel Daniel Parke Custis?

11. Which state is the birthplace of the most U.S. presidents?

12. Who was the first man defeated in a presidential election?

13. The 8th, 9th and 10th presidents served in office in the same year. What was the year and who were they?

14. Who was the father-in-law of Confederate President Jefferson Davis?

15. What does the S in Harry S Truman's name stand for?

16. He wrote his own epitaph, describing himself as having been the founder of the University of Virginia among other things, but not once did he refer to himself as President of the United States. Who is he?

17. What state capital's maiden name was Lancaster, but was renamed after the son of a woman whose maiden name was Nancy Hanks?

18. What President and First Lady were fifth cousins?

19. Who holds the record for most places named after him in the U.S.?

20. How many Presidents of the United States are not buried in America?

# Answers—The Presidency

1. *He didn't have one.*

2 . *John Adams and Thomas Jefferson.*

3. *Calvin Coolidge, in 1872.*

4. *The Blair House (The White House was undergoing renovation at the time).*

5. *Macaroni.*

6. *Herbert Hoover.*

7. *Gerald Ford.*

8. *$25,000.*

9. *14 years (and you must be a natural born citizen of the U.S.).*

10. *Martha Washington.*

11. *Virginia (8).*

12. *Thomas Jefferson (He lost to John Adams—George Washington ran unopposed).*

13. *1841— Martin Van Buren, William Henry Harrison, John Tyler.*

14. *Zachary Taylor.*

15. *Nothing. Truman's folks couldn't settle on a name, so they just gave him an initial.*

16. *Thomas Jefferson.*

17. *Lincoln, Nebraska.*

18. *Franklin Delano Roosevelt and Eleanor Roosevelt.*

19. *George Washington (257 townships, 121 cities, towns, and villages, 33 counties; and 1 state).*

20. *An old trick question that's been dug up—Five presidents are not buried in America (or anywhere else)—Ford, Carter, Reagan, Bush and Clinton.*

• • • • • •

The number of left-handed men, for some unknown reason, is double that of left-handed women.

• • • • • •

The tombstone of Gail Borden, the founder of Borden's dairy products, is in the shape of a can of condensed milk.

---

## Trivia Test

What is the most popular street name in the United States?

*Park.*

Droplets of moisture from a sneeze can travel as far as twelve feet and as fast as 100 miles per hour.

• • • • • •

Your tongue is the only muscle in your body that's attached at only one end.

• • • • • •

275 pound watermelons have been known to grow along the banks of the Tigris River in Turkey.

• • • • • •

## Bathroom Trivia

It was during the 1970's when a New York City police officer accidentally shot himself in the leg as he was dropping his gunbelt and pants in the bathroom of a Brooklyn station house. In the interest of law and order, he shall remain nameless.

• • • • • •

President U.S. Grant ate cucumbers for breakfast.

• • • • • •

Where there's smoke there's *lunt*. That's what the fume from a pipe is called.

• • • • • •

If you have three quarters, four dimes, and four pennies, you have $1.19. You also have the largest amount of money in coins without being able to make change for a dollar.

• • • • • •

Honeybees are deaf. Say what? Yes, and so are turtles.

• • • • • •

*Sheik* means "old man" in Arabic.

• • • • • •

Wall Street got its name in 1654 when residents of New York
built a wooden blockade across that area of lower Manhattan
to protect against a possible attack by Indians.

• • • • • •

The letters M.G. on the British sports car stand for Morris
Garage.

• • • • • •

*The Lawrence Welk Show* was originally called the *Dodge
Dancing Party*.

• • • • • •

Calvin Coolidge's will was one sentence long.

• • • • • •

Babies up to seven months old can breathe and swallow at
the same time.

---

## Trivia Test

Who played for the last time at Candlestick Park in
San Francisco on August 29, 1966?

*Candlestick Park, August 29, 1966 marked the last
performance of The Beatles.*

---

One of the primary reasons the Mayflower Pilgrims ended
their voyage at Plymouth Rock was because they ran out of
beer.

• • • • • •

You have to count all the way to one thousand before the
letter "a" is used in spelling a number.

• • • • • •

Fireflies light up as a means of sexual attraction. The brightness and the frequency of flickering supposedly identify the opposite sexes to one another.

• • • • • •

"Forty" is the only number in English which, when spelled out, has all its letters in alphabetical order.

• • • • • •

If you've had a bellyful, you've had about two quarts. That's the average adult's stomach capacity.

• • • • • •

A world class high jumper could clear the bar at almost fifty feet on the moon.

• • • • • •

Most of the books you own will disintegrate within the next fifty years unless they are printed on acid-proof stock.

• • • • • •

The World Trade Center in New York City has 43,600 windows.

• • • • • •

Seals have been known to swim for as long as eight months and as far as 6,000 miles without touching land.

• • • • • •

British naval hero Horatio Nelson had a chronic case of seasickness.

• • • • • •

An ant's sense of smell is comparable to a dog's.

• • • • • •

The space between your nostrils is called your *columella.*

• • • • • •

William Shakespeare has no living descendants.

• • • • • •

It takes about 150 dead ermines to make one ermine coat.

• • • • • •

Comedian Albert Brooks' real name is Albert Einstein.

• • • • • •

If all the oceans evaporated, Hawaii would be the tallest mountain in the world.

• • • • • •

Honey is used in antifreeze mixes.

• • • • • •

Thomas Edison wanted to put a large phonograph in the mouth of the Statue of Liberty to give it a voice that could be heard all over New York Harbor. His idea was met with silence.

• • • • • •

## Bathroom Trivia

Jerry Lewis got mad at his agent one day and reportedly had the agent's picture plastered on toilet paper rolls.

• • • • • •

Dog meat is a delicacy in China. So is bird's nest soup.

• • • • • •

Robert Earl Hughes was the world's heaviest human being, tipping the scales at 1,067 pounds.

• • • • • •

Bill McCoy was a rumrunner who brought the top of the line in booze to the U.S. from the West Indies. His stuff was so good that a new expression was coined—*the real McCoy.*

• • • • • •

# Setting The Record Straight

Shooting stars are not stars. They are meteors.

Black-eyed peas are not peas. They are beans.

The flying fox is not a fox. It is a bat.

Catgut string does not come from a cat. It is from a sheep's intestines.

The Canary Islands were not named after canaries. They were named after a breed of dogs (Canariae insulae).

The Douglas fir is not a fir. It is a pine tree.

The Pennsylvania Dutch are not Dutch. They are German.

The kangaroo rat is not a rat. It is a gopher.

The silkworm is not a worm. It is a caterpillar.

Blackboard chalk is not chalk. It is plaster of Paris.

St. Patrick was not Irish. He was born in Britain.

The pineapple is not pine and it's not an apple. It is a berry.

A prairie dog is not a dog. It is a rodent.

Turkeys are not from Turkey. They are from North America.

A horned toad is not a toad. It is a lizard.

A guinea pig is not a pig. It is a rodent.

A peanut is not a nut. It is a legume.

A ladybird is not a bird. It is a beetle.

A banana tree is not a tree. It is an herb.

• • • • • •

# Mapping It Out

A Geography Quiz

1. What do the following ten places have in common: Atlanta, Cleveland, Dayton, Hartford, Jacksonville, New Haven, Newark, Norfolk, Philadelphia and Phoenix?

2. Where was Kentucky Fried Chicken's Colonel Sanders born?

3. Name the languages spoken in the three countries closest to the U.S.

4. What country celebrates Thanksgiving on the second Monday of October?

5. Where is the world's largest garbage dump?

6. Alaska and Hawaii were the 49th and 50th states of the U.S. Which was 48th?

7. Constantinople, Edo, and Ft. Dearborn are former names of what three cities?

8. Where is the only place in the world you can see the sun rise on the Pacific and set on the Atlantic?

9. Name the only state in the U.S. that borders on Canadian territory.

10. In what country is Pepsi Cola spelled NENCN-KONA?

*Answers next page*

# **Answers—Mapping It Out**

1. *They are all towns in New York.*

2. *Indiana.*

3. *English, Spanish and Russian.*

4. *Canada.*

5. *Staten Island, N.Y.*

6. *Arizona.*

7. *Istanbul, Tokyo, and Chicago.*

8. *The Panama Canal—where the Pacific is east of the Atlantic.*

9. *Alaska—all the others border on "provinces".*

10. *Russia.*

Bathroom Quote—"If I had been technically trained, I would have quit."—King Camp Gillette, on spending eight arduous years inventing the safety razor.

• • • • • •

The only four letter word that ends in "e-n-y" is *deny*.

• • • • • •

Robert E. Lee was buried barefoot in 1870 because the coffin was too small to allow for his boots.

• • • • • •

A flea expert is a pullicologist.

• • • • • •

The expression to *mind your p's and q's* comes from old English pubs, when bartenders kept track of how much a customer drank by the pints and quarts in front of them.

• • • • • •

## Bathroom Trivia

The electric razor made its debut on the American marketplace March 18, 1931. It should be noted that, until any kind of razor was invented, man shaved by pulling hairs out individually or by cutting them with sharp-edged stones.

• • • • • •

General Custer's soldiers called him *Hard Ass*.

• • • • • •

Aviator Orville Wright was expelled for mischievous behavior from the Richmond, Indiana grammar school during the sixth grade in 1883.

• • • • • •

Ping-Pong is the national sport of China.

• • • • • •

A bear has 42 teeth.

• • • • • •

A five year U.S. Public Health Service study discovered that kissing can cause tooth decay.

• • • • • •

Half of the peanuts grown in America are used for peanut butter.

• • • • • •

Female armadillos have exactly four babies at a time and they are always the same sex.

• • • • • •

The one hundred dollar bill is the largest denomination of currency now issued. Larger denominations were discontinued in 1969 because of limited use and are now being phased out of circulation.

• • • • • •

Leonardo da Vinci could draw with one hand and write with the other at the same time.

• • • • • •

A kangaroo can hop along at a clip of 40 miles per hour.

• • • • • •

When asked to name a number from 1 to 10, the most frequently given answer is "5".

• • • • • •

# Cover To Cover

John Travolta was the first man to appear on the cover of *McCall's* magazine in July 1978 ... *TV Guide's* first edition in 1953 featured Lucille Ball and her newborn son, Desi Arnaz IV, on the cover ... The Virgin Mary has appeared on the front of *Time* magazine more than any other woman—10 ... *Time's* first Man of the Year was Charles A. Lindbergh, in 1927 ... Mia Farrow was the cover feature of *People* magazine's first issue in 1974.

• • • • • •

The average American drinks three and a half cups of coffee a day.

• • • • • •

Bathroom Quote—Iran's Ayatollah Khomeini, on going to the bathroom, gave this edict to his Moslem constituents: "... one must squat in such a way as not to be turning one's back on Mecca."

• • • • • •

If you're interested in this book, you just might be a *spermologer*—a collector of trivia.

• • • • • •

Mark Twain served in the Confederate Army for all of one week. Then he deserted.

• • • • • •

## Bathroom Trivia

The first brushless shaving cream in America was Burma Shave. As pre-baby boomers may remember, it was popularly promoted with roadside jingles, a series of highway billboards about 100 feet apart, each containing one line of a verse like the following: "Within this vale/Of toil and sin/Your head grows bald/But not your chin/Burma-Shave."

• • • • • •

The average American gets 410 pieces of mail a year.

• • • • • •

---

# Trivia Test

Name the Seven Seas.

*There are no specific "seven seas." It is an expression meaning all the oceans and seas of the world.*

---

• • • • • •

Philanthropist Andrew Carnegie promised his mother that he'd never marry while she was alive. Carnegie's mother died when he was 51. He married a year later.

• • • • • •

## Bathroom Trivia

In the high mountains of Sumdah, India young children wear pants without seats until they become toilet-trained.

• • • • • •

Table tennis balls have been known to travel off the paddle at speeds up to 105.6 miles per hour.

• • • • • •

The precise translation of the French term *pot pourri* is *putrid pot.*

• • • • • •

Composer Johann Sebastian Bach was quite a father—to the tune of 20 children.

• • • • • •

## Bathroom Trivia

Country star Tammy Wynette's 17,500 square foot home in Nashville, Tennessee has 15 bathrooms.

• • • • • •

Statistics show that Americans drive an average 206.2 miles per week.

• • • • • •

Boca Raton, one of Florida's posh resorts, is Spanish for the *mouse's mouth.*

• • • • • •

Northern General Ulysses S. Grant and his wife, Julia, owned slaves who were not freed until after the Civil War had ended.

• • • • • •

A frog has to close its eyes in order to swallow.

• • • • • •

Timekeepers have clocked the action time in a 60 minute football game to be 14 minutes.

• • • • • •

When the first White House telephone rang in the 1880's, President Grover Cleveland answered it himself.

• • • • • •

Novelist Leon Uris dropped out of high school to join the Marines.

• • • • • •

# Last Names, First Names

Mason & Dixon, surveyors          Charles and Jeremiah

Smith Brothers,                          William and Andrew
cough drop makers          (William is pictured above "Trade"
                                 and Andrew above "Mark"
                                 on the cough drop box.)

Lewis and Clark, expeditioners     Meriwether and William

The Brothers Grimm, authors          Jacob and Wilhelm

Baskin & Robbins, ice               Burton and Irving
cream manufacturer

Rolls-Royce, auto manufacturer     Charles and Frederick

H. & R. Block, tax advisors          Henry and Richard

Brooks Brothers, clothiers            Henry and Daniel

Sears & Roebuck,                    Richard and Alvah
department store chain

• • • • • •

A college professor conducted a study of fingernail biting in 1978 and found that up to 15 percent of Americans also chew their toenails.

• • • • • •

## Bathroom Trivia

In 1840, poet Henry Wadsworth Longfellow became the first American to have plumbing installed in his home.

## Trivia Test

The year 1961 reads the same upside down. When's the next year that will happen again?

*6009*

Pigs can run a 7 ½ minute mile.

• • • • • •

A typical American hospital has three to four times more employees than patients.

• • • • • •

If "beauty is only skin deep", it can't be more than 3/16 of an inch thick.

• • • • • •

The federal withholding tax taken out of your paycheck was enacted as a "temporary" wartime measure.

• • • • • •

The Hawaiian alphabet has only twelve letters a,e,h,i,k,l,m,n,o,p,u and w.

• • • • • •

The longest running television show is *Meet The Press*. It's been on the air since November 20, 1947.

• • • • • •

Sioux Indian Chief Crazy Horse was called Curly as a kid.

• • • • • •

Benjamin Franklin was the fifteenth child of a Boston soapmaker.

• • • • • •

The father of writer Hart Crane is the creator of Life Savers candy—Clarence Crane.

• • • • • •

The turkey is widely regarded as the dumbest domesticated animal.

• • • • • •

An inch-thick rope of spider's silk can withstand up to 148,000 pounds of pressure.

• • • • • •

## Bathroom Trivia

Surveys show that the majority of American men would rather shower than bathe, but it's a 50-50 proposition among women.

• • • • • •

In 1968 there were 5 million-dollar lottery winners around the U.S. who didn't claim their tickets.

• • • • • •

There are five times as many rats in Lima, Peru as there are people.

• • • • • •

The Bowie knife was not invented by James Bowie of Alamo fame. It was invented by his brother, Rezin Pleasant Bowie.

• • • • • •

Someone conducted a study which concluded that stewardesses have the lowest divorce rate among working women.

• • • • • •

A horse can look forward with one eye and back with the other.

• • • • • •

In most cases, it's cheaper to send a student to college than it is to keep a prisoner in jail.

• • • • • •

Jellyfish sometimes evaporate.

• • • • • •

# The Little Known About The Well Known

Former president Jimmy Carter has flat feet. He rolled his arches over a Coke bottle every day until they were sufficiently curved to pass his physical for the Naval Academy.

● ● ● ● ● ●

Gangster Al Capone's business card listed him as a "secondhand furniture dealer".

● ● ● ● ● ●

Adolph Hitler was *Time* magazine's Man of the Year for 1938.

● ● ● ● ● ●

The first chewing gum was brought to the U.S. by Mexican commander Santa Anna when he visited New York in 1859.

● ● ● ● ● ●

Two-heads-are better-than-one-dept.— Jonathan Swift, the author of *Gulliver's Travels,* shares his grave at St. Patrick's Cathedral in Dublin with the skull of an unknown person.

● ● ● ● ● ●

Walter Cronkite was a college dropout. He left the University of Texas in his junior year to work for the *Houston Post.*

● ● ● ● ● ●

Frankie Avalon held his nose while singing *Dee Dee Dinah,* his first hit song.

● ● ● ● ● ●

American naval hero John Paul Jones wound up his career as an admiral in the Russian navy.

● ● ● ● ● ●

George Washington was scared to death that he'd be buried alive. Just before he died, he demanded his body be kept above ground for a few days in the event he might come to.

. . . . . .

Diane Keaton won an Oscar for her film portrayal of the title role in *Annie Hall.* Her real last name is Hall.

. . . . . .

Balboa, the discoverer of the Pacific Ocean, was falsely accused of treason and beheaded in 1517.

. . . . . .

One of Rudyard Kipling's famous works is *Road to Mandalay.* He was never there.

. . . . . .

The grandfather of Charles Lindbergh changed the family's last name. If he hadn't, our high flying hero would've been known as Charles Manson.

. . . . . .

J.C. Penney's middle name was Cash.

. . . . . .

Former first lady Betty Ford, whose maiden name is Betty Bloomer, was sometimes called "Betty Pants" by her Grand Rapids, Michigan schoolmates.

. . . . . .

Actor, writer, director and producer Michael Landon, an all around television wizard, wasn't such a wiz academically. In his Collingswood, N.J. high school class, Landon reportedly graduated 300th out of a total of 301 students.

. . . . . .

President Andrew Johnson's wife taught him how to read and write.

. . . . . .

It's not certain if that was his inspiration, but Robert Louis Stevenson was on his honeymoon when he wrote *Travels with a Donkey*.

•  •  •  •  •  •

Preacher Billy Graham was once considered the best Fuller Brush salesman in North Carolina.

•  •  •  •  •  •

In 1936 Zsa Zsa Gabor was crowned Miss Hungary but had to give up the title when it was discovered she wasn't old enough to meet the minimum age requirement—16.

•  •  •  •  •  •

•  •  •  •  •  •

*Utopia* is an ancient Greek word meaning "nowhere".

•  •  •  •  •  •

In 1862 *Les Misérables* author Victor Hugo was vacationing and anxious to know how his new novel was doing, so he wrote to his publisher: "?" The reply was: "!"

•  •  •  •  •  •

## Bathroom Trivia

Casanova journeyed with a custom-made portable bath—for two, of course.

•  •  •  •  •  •

Dolphins have bigger brains than humans.

•  •  •  •  •  •

# One Day Wonders

*Can you identify the fleeting claim to fame of these people?*

1. Robert Opel

2. Leon Czolgosz

3. Margaret Gorman

4. Sal Durante

5. Soeur Sourire

6. George Willig

7. Victoria May Bodinger

8. Yuri Gagarin

9. Charles Guiteau

10. Maria Cruz

*Answers Next Page*

# Answers—One Day Wonders

1.   *He streaked The Academy Awards in 1973—as David Niven, on stage at the time, ad-libbed, the man who displayed his "shortcomings".*

2.   *Assassin of President William McKinley.*

3.   *First Miss America, crowned September 7, 1921. Gorman was 15 years old, stood 5'1", and had measurements of 30-25-32.*

4.   *The fan who caught Roger Maris' 61st homerun in 1961.*

5.   *The Singing Nun, famous for one hit recording, "Dominique".*

6.   *He climbed the south tower of the World Trade Center in New York City on May 26, 1977. Abraham Beame, then mayor, fined him $1.10—a penny for each floor of the building.*

7.   *Miss Vicky. She married Tiny Tim on "The Tonight Show", December 17, 1969.*

8.   *Russian cosmonaut who was the first man in space, April 12, 1961.*

9.   *Some grave bathroom trivia. Guiteau came out of the men's room of a Washington train station and shot President James Garfield, July 2, 1881. Garfield died September 19, 1881. Guiteau was hanged the following June.*

10.  *Acting on Marlon Brando's behalf at the Academy Awards ceremonies, Maria Cruz, using the Indian name Sasheen Littlefeather, refused the Oscar for Brando's performance in "The Godfather", citing injustices to the American Indian.*

A golf hole is four inches deep.

* * * * * *

The literal translation of *hors d'oeuvre* is *outside the work.*

* * * * * *

The almost extinct giant tortoise of the Galapagos Islands lives longer than any other animal. The 600 pounder can live to be 200 years old.

* * * * * *

Clark Gable's first name was William. His middle name was Clark.

* * * * * *

In Washington, D.C. no building can be constructed taller than the Capitol.

* * * * * *

Presidents Grant, Taft, Hoover and Eisenhower never held any other elective office.

* * * * * *

Rabbits talk to each other by thumping their feet.

* * * * * *

The oldest known vegetable is the pea, used by the Chinese as far back as 2,000 B.C.

* * * * * *

That sound you hear in the seashell when you hold it up to your ear is not from the shell. It's the echo of the blood pulsing in your ear.

• • • • • •

Beavers can swim underwater for fifteen minutes.

• • • • • •

Llamas have extremely bad breath.

• • • • • •

In the 1700's, a trapper could sell the deerskin of a buck for a dollar—hence, the term *buck*.

• • • • • •

France's King Louis XIV was on the throne so long that he was succeeded by his great-grandson.

• • • • • •

The official state sport of Maryland is jousting.

• • • • • •

A cucumber is 96 percent water.

• • • • • •

Some grasshoppers and crickets have hearing organs on their legs.

• • • • • •

A dime has 118 ridges around it.

• • • • • •

Elephants are taught to like peanuts. They eat no peanuts in the wild.

• • • • • •

Hugh Hefner was going to call his magazine Stag Party but a friend convinced him to name it *Playboy*.

• • • • • •

The ridges on corduroy are called wales.

• • • • • •

There are eleven time zones in Russia.

• • • • • •

Fish can become seasick if kept on board a ship.

• • • • • •

A little birdie gave Bertha Diugi the idea for the invention of the parakeet diaper.

• • • • • •

The average American carries four credit cards.

• • • • • •

## Bathroom Trivia

In England long ago, if people had something to stew about, it was good, clean fun. A public bath was called a stew during the reign of Henry II.

• • • • • •

In answer to that question you never knew you wondered about—yes, a fetus in the womb can get hiccups.

• • • • • •

Kentucky Fried Chicken's Colonel Sanders once tried to claim his white suits as a tax deduction but the IRS wouldn't allow it.

• • • • • •

A flea can jump more than a foot—comparable to a human leaping over the Washington Monument with plenty to spare.

• • • • • •

Deep throat dept.—As you might have guessed, giraffes are very susceptible to throat infections.

• • • • • •

We may see a *man in the moon* but the Chinese think they see a *rabbit*.

• • • • • •

Adolf Hitler's favorite movie was *King Kong*.

• • • • • •

The Mormon Tabernacle Church in Salt Lake City, Utah was built without any nails.

• • • • • •

In tennis, the term "love", meaning zero, comes from the French *l'oeuf* which is an egg, as in goose egg.

• • • • • •

An old *World Telegram* newspaper experiment determined that, in golf, the exact odds against scoring a hole-in-one on a par three hole are 8,750 to 1.

• • • • • •

President Zachary Taylor never voted in a presidential election—not even his own.

• • • • • •

Inventor Thomas Edison never graduated from grade school. Neither did literary greats Mark Twain, Charles Dickens, or Noel Coward.

● ● ● ● ● ●

If Superman is faster than a speeding bullet, he travels at better than 4,000 feet per second—the speed of a bullet from a .22 caliber rifle.

● ● ● ● ● ●

## Loose Change

If a coin has the letter "S" printed on it, it was minted in San Francisco; a "D" means it was made in Denver; and no letter at all denotes that it was minted in Philadelphia.

The odds against a flipped coin coming up with the same side showing ten times in a row are 1,023 to 1.

The mill, equal to one-tenth of a cent, was declared the lowest money of account by Congress in 1786, but was never minted.

It cost a penny for a man to walk across the Brooklyn Bridge when it opened on May 21, 1883. There was a two cent charge for sheep.

"E Pluribus Unum", the Latin expression appearing on U.S. currency, means "one out of many".

The town of Cash, Texas was named in honor of its first postmaster, J.A. Money.

If you look closely at a Franklin Delano Roosevelt dime, under FDR's head you'll find the initials J.S. for its designer, John Spinnock.

Abraham Lincoln was carrying Confederate money when he was assassinated.

The shell is 12 percent of the weight of the entire egg.

•  •  •  •  •  •

A 1982 survey found that 38 percent of people in the U.S. watch television during dinner.

•  •  •  •  •  •

The size of a polo field is 12.4 acres, the biggest playing field in sports.

•  •  •  •  •  •

Wrangall, Alaska has the highest zip code of any city in the U.S.—99929. Agawam, Massachusetts has the lowest—01001.

•  •  •  •  •  •

Mark Twain was the first to type a book manuscript. Working on Remington Model No. 1 which he bought in 1874, Twain typed at a speed of 19 words per minute.

•  •  •  •  •  •

Men outnumber women in prison by 25 to 1 in the U. S.

•  •  •  •  •  •

In 1896 Henry C. Traute came up with the phrase that appears on all matchbook covers—"Close before striking".

•  •  •  •  •  •

Louisiana's city of Baton Rouge is a French term meaning *red stick*.

•  •  •  •  •  •

## Trivia Test

What do the letters S-O-S, as in "help", stand for?

*S-O-S doesn't stand for anything. The letters were chosen for Morse Code as a distress signal because of their simplicity—three dots, three dashes and three dots.*

Smith is the most common last name in the U.S. Rounding out the top ten, in order, are Johnson, Williams, Brown, Jones, Miller, Davis, Wilson, Anderson and Taylor.

• • • • • •

Liberace once used the stage name Walter Busterkeys.

• • • • • •

The Oreo is the world's bestselling cookie. Over five billion are sold every year—and that's just in America.

• • • • • •

Paul Revere took his midnight ride on a horse named Brown Beauty.

• • • • • •

In China, the day a child is born it is considered one year old.

• • • • • •

### Bathroom Trivia

Only 51 disposable Gillette razors (at five dollars apiece) were sold in the company's first year, 1903. By 1906, however, 300,000 razor sets and close to 500,000 blades were purchased.

• • • • • •

There are 1,792 steps to the top of the Eiffel Tower, 296 steps to the top of the Leaning Tower of Pisa, and 168 steps to the crown of the Statue of Liberty.

• • • • • •

Dr. Scholl's first name is William.

• • • • • •

An armadillo can be housebroken.

• • • • • •

Rudyard Kipling would write only with black ink.

• • • • • •

In many species of birds, the eyes weigh more than the brain.

• • • • • •

New Mexico is the only state with two official languages— English and Spanish.

• • • • • •

Parrots have a particularly keen sense of hearing. During World War I, a group of them were kept on top of the Eiffel Tower in Paris to hear the sound of planes and warn of the approaching aircraft.

• • • • • •

Lightning is the cause of most forest fires.

• • • • • •

In case anyone asks you to name all of the letters on an eye chart, here they are: c,d,e,f,l,o,p,t and z.

• • • • • •

The maximum weight for a golf ball is 1.62 oz.

• • • • • •

Napoleon's body lies in Paris today, but when he died in 1821 at St. Helena, he was buried underneath a tombstone which read "Here lies ..." No name was engraved.

• • • • • •

# Initially Speaking

*Abbreviations and what they stand for*

J&B (scotch)—Justerini and Brooks.

STP (oil treatment)—Scientifically Treated Petroleum.

P.F. Flyers (sneakers)—Posture Foundation.

K-Mart (chain store)—Kresge, for its founder, Sebastian S. Kresge.

TNT (explosive)—Trinitrotuluene.

EPCOT (amusement park)—Experimental Prototype Community of Tomorrow.

A.M. (morning hours)—ante meridiem (from Latin "before midday").

P.M. (afternoon and evening)—post meridiem (from Latin "after midday").

FIAT (automobile)—Fabricana Italiana Automobile Torino (Italian Automobile Factory at Torino).

*QBVII* (book)—Queen's Bench 7 (The title of this Leon Uris novel refers to the courtroom.)

At the Port Royal Golf Course in Bermuda on March 27,1975 twenty-one year old Joe Flynn recorded the lowest 18 hole score ever, an 82. If you think those statistics might not be up to par, Flynn's 18 hole mark was for throwing the ball.

• • • • • •

Cinderella is known as *Tuna* in Finland.

• • • • • •

In days of long ago, when railroad men patronized brothels, they left their red lamps outside—such was the derivation of the *red light district.*

• • • • • •

Only one word can be formed by rearranging the letters of the word "chesty"—*scythe.*

• • • • • •

A duck feather weighs approximately .016 to .063 grams.

• • • • • •

Before 1859, baseball umpires sat behind home plate in rocking chairs.

• • • • • •

The term "senator" comes from the Latin *senex* which means "old man".

• • • • • •

Earthworms do not have eyes or ears.

• • • • • •

A Federal Aviation Administration study found that the average airline stewardess has a nose 2.18 inches long.

• • • • • •

Insects can shiver.

• • • • • •

The Campbell's Soup red and white label derives from the colors of the Cornell University football team.

• • • • • •

The covering on the back of a chair is an *antimacasser*—from "Macassar" which was a popular hair oil.

---

## Trivia Test

What hero is honored with a statue in Crystal City, Texas?

*Popeye.*

---

College grads now earn a master's degree in two or three year programs, but until 1869, the M.A. was an honorary award.

• • • • • •

The Finnish term *saippuakauppias* means "soap seller" in English. Spell it backwards and, palindromically, you wind up with the same word.

• • • • • •

The odds are 423-1 against becoming a millionaire in the U.S.

• • • • • •

The "D" in D-Day stands for "Day" to reiterate its military importance.

• • • • • •

A bee uses 22 muscles to sting someone.

• • • • • •

To mathematicians, the earth shapes up as an *oblate spheroid.*

• • • • • •

East St. Louis is in Illinois.

• • • • • •

The Parker Bros. game company prints more play money in a year—$18,500,000,000,000— than the total sum of real money printed in the whole world.

• • • • • •

A basketball hoop is 18 inches in diameter.

• • • • • •

In Kansas, New Jersey, Rhode Island and South Carolina a woman can legally get married at the age of 12.

• • • • • •

## Bathroom Trivia

Credit, or blame, Charles N. Van Cleave for the pay toilet. His invention of the coin-operated lock in 1910 made it possible to pay as you go.

• • • • • •

The stopwatch seen on television's *60 Minutes* is made by Heuer.

• • • • • •

BMW, as in the car, stands for Bavarian Motor Works.

• • • • • •

Two of three Americans have hemorrhoids.

• • • • • •

# Tube Test

1. In *The Honeymooners*, what was Alice Kramden's maiden name?

2. Who was the first mystery guest to appear on *What's My Line?* And the last?

3. Who hosted *Death Valley Days* in 1965 and 1966?

4. What do the initials U.N.C.L.E. stand for in the *Man From U.N.C.L.E.?*

5. Who sings *The Love Boat* theme song?

6. What couple lived at 148 Bonnie Meadow Drive, New Rochelle, N.Y.?

7. Dr. Francis Horwich was the host of what television show?

8. What was the real name of the original Morris the Cat of commercial fame?

9. Walter Annenberg founded it in 1953 and soon after it became the best-selling product of its kind. What is it?

10. Mechanical mouse Topo Gigio was a frequent guest on *The Ed Sullivan Show*. Who was Topo's girlfriend?

*Answers next page*

# Tube Test Answers

1. *Gibson.*

2. *Baseball's Phil Rizzuto was the first to appear. For its finale, the longtime host of "What's My Line?", John Daly, was the mystery guest.*

3. *Ronald Reagan.*

4. *United Network Command for Law Enforcement.*

5. *Jack Jones.*

6. *Rob and Laura Petrie of "The Dick Van Dyke Show".*

7. *"Ding Dong School". She was Miss Francis.*

8. *Lucky.*

9. *"TV Guide".*

10. *Rosy.*

An ant has five noses.

• • • • • •

Chanel No. 5 perfume got its name because France introduced it on the fifth day of the fifth month of 1951 and because "5" was Coco Chanel's lucky number.

• • • • • •

The T.I.D. often found on a doctor's prescription stands for *ter in die*, a Latin term meaning "three times a day".

• • • • • •

At one time, all radio stations east of the Mississippi River had call letters beginning with the letter "W". West of the Mississippi, they began with the letter "K".

• • • • • •

A cave man's life span was only 18 years.

• • • • • •

The home team must provide the referee with 24 footballs for each National Football League game.

• • • • • •

In colonial Boston schoolteachers earned about seven cents a day.

• • • • • •

Giraffes can't swim.

• • • • • •

Even horses have stage names. The real name of television's Mr. Ed was Bamboo Harvester.

• • • • • •

Jim Hogg, the governor of Texas from 1891 to 1895, named his only daughter "Ima".

• • • • • •

Actor Stewart Granger was born James Stewart.

• • • • • •

Cats can't taste sweet things.

• • • • • •

The pilgrims had planned on coming to America in two ships, the *Mayflower* and the *Speedwell* but the *Speedwell* was not considered seaworthy enough.

• • • • • •

The only brothers to sign the *Declaration of Independence* were Richard Henry Lee and Francis Lightfoot Lee.

• • • • • •

The Bank of America was originally called The Bank of Italy.

• • • • • •

## Bathroom Trivia

According to the latest government census, 2.2 percent of American households do not have complete plumbing facilities.

• • • • • •

The working title of Joseph Heller's 1961 novel *Catch-22* was *Catch-18*.

• • • • • •

# Playing The Percentages

40 percent of Americans suffer from shyness ... Only about 5 percent of people who are blind were born that way ... 99 percent of the people in the U.S. own a television set. . . 99.9 percent have a toaster ... 70 percent of the earth is covered by water, but less than 1 percent of that is drinkable ... About 65 percent of your body is water . . . As much as 90 percent of a tree is made up of air with the rest minerals from the soil ... A gorilla sleeps away 70 percent of its twenty-three year life span ... The bathroom is the scene of 3 percent of all accidents in the home ... The bedroom tops the accident-by-room rate at 40 percent.

● ● ● ● ● ●

The world's tallest "structure", at 2,120 feet, is the tower of Warszarwa Radio in Poland. Chicago's Sears Tower, 110 stories and 1,454 feet, is the world's tallest "building".

---

## Trivia Test

Lloyd Copeland is credited with the initial development of the microwave oven. Who is his famous granddaughter?

*Linda Ronstadt.*

---

Ben Franklin coined the word "battery".

● ● ● ● ● ●

A newborn baby cannot shed tears.

● ● ● ● ● ●

An adult's skin weighs approximately six pounds.

● ● ● ● ● ●

Would you believe that a fifteen letter word, with no letters the same, is *uncopyrightable?*

• • • • • •

Only right-handed players can play polo according to the U.S Polo Association. The governing body made the ruling in 1974 to cut down on collisions between lefties and righties as they ride on horses to hit a wooden bag with their sticks.

• • • • • •

Eugenio Pacelli, Angelo Giuseppe Roncalli, Giovanni Battista Montini, and Albino Luciani—do you know these famous Italians? Of course you do. They are, respectively, Pope Pius XII, Pope John XXIII, Pope Paul VI, and Pope John Paul I— the four Popes who preceded the current Pontiff, Karol Wojtyla—Pope John Paul II.

• • • • • •

The little rubber gizmo on the end of a toothbrush is called a *stimulator tip.*

• • • • • •

In 1930 Fred Newton became the only man ever to swim the Mississippi River—lengthwise (1,826 miles over a six month period).

• • • • • •

France's King Louis XIV bathed only once a year.

• • • • • •

Rock star Jimi Hendrix was working on the song *The Story of Life* the night he died.

• • • • • •

After World War I, German money was almost useless and was cheaper to burn than firewood.

• • • • • •

# It's Against The Law

*... Old and odd laws around the U.S.—some of which may still be on the books!*

In Portland, Oregon a priest or minister is not allowed to perform a wedding ceremony at a skating rink.

It's against the law for frogs to croak after 11 p.m. in Memphis, Tennessee.

A Lexington, Kentucky law says that you are not permitted to carry ice cream cones in your pocket.

Barbers are not allowed to eat onions between 7 a.m. and 7 p.m. in Waterloo, Nebraska.

It's against the law to sing out of tune in North Carolina.

You'd be breaking the law if you tickled a girl's chin with a feather duster in Portland, Maine.

A Baldwin Park, California statute forbids riding a bike in a swimming pool.

In Wilbur, Washington it's illegal to ride an ugly horse.

It's against the law to open a massage parlor in Horneytown, North Carolina.

A Texas ordinance has it that when two trains meet at a railroad crossing, both must come to a stop. Then, neither train can continue until the other one is out of sight.

A survey says that the least-liked vegetable is the turnip.

• • • • • •

The bare facts—a two-year test by the American Heart Association found that only 7 percent of nudist camp residents suffered from high blood pressure compared to a national average of 17 percent.

• • • • • •

Most snakes can go without eating for a whole year.

• • • • • •

Way back when, tombstones were first placed on plots over the dead so that the deceased could not come out and harm the living.

• • • • • •

Most monkeys are near-sighted.

• • • • • •

The U.S.A.'s gold is kept at Ft. Knox, but do you know where the country's silver is kept?—West Point.

---

### Trivia Test

In Hyde Park, N.Y. the CIA stands for something other than the Central Intelligence Agency. What?

*Culinary Institute of America.*

---

Hockey is called *shinny* in Scotland.

• • • • • •

There are 88 keys on a piano—52 white and 36 black.

• • • • • •

The Manhattan cocktail, a concoction of whiskey and sweet vermouth, was created by Winston Churchill's mother.

• • • • • •

Albert Einstein's last words were spoken in German. Since the attending nurse did not know the language, we'll never know what he said.

• • • • • •

A termite can live thirty years.

• • • • • •

Kilts originated in France, not Scotland.

• • • • • •

A snail takes 115 days to travel a mile.

• • • • • •

*Dr. Jekyll and Mr. Hyde* was the result of a Robert Louis Stevenson dream. In fact, Stevenson said he was able to dream plots for his stories whenever he felt like it.

• • • • • •

## Bathroom Trivia

On April 23, 1978 a 25 pound green iceberg fell from the sky and landed in Ripley, Tennessee. The Federal Aviation Administration later reported that the ice mass was frozen waste that had fallen from a leaky airplane toilet.

• • • • • •

According to ancient Hindu law, the punishment for adultery was the removal of one's nose.

• • • • • •

Forty million Ritz crackers are bought every day.

• • • • • •

Teddy Roosevelt had four sons. Three of them were killed serving their country during wartime.

• • • • • •

A giraffe can kill a lion with one swift kick.

• • • • • •

# The Fear Of It

*"The only thing we have to fear is fear itself." Franklin Delano Roosevelt's words are an apt description of "phobobia"—a fear of fears. If you're afraid to look into a bathroom mirror, that's "eisoptrophobia" ... And if you're a bibliophobic, you wouldn't even be reading this. "Bibliophobia" is a fear of books.*

Here are some more:

| Phobia | Fear |
|---|---|
| batophobia | walking |
| blennophobia | slime |
| chrometophobia | money |
| clinophobia | beds |
| ergophobia | work |
| gametophobia | marriage |
| hippophobia | horses |
| homichlophobia | fog |
| keraunophobia | thunder |
| kyphophobia | stooping |
| mysophobia | dirt |
| ombrophobia | rain |
| phagophobia | swallowing |
| pogonophobia | beards |
| sitophobia | food |
| thixophobia | touching |
| tropophobia | making changes |
| vestiophobia | clothing |

• • • • • •

Pablo Diego José Francisco do Paula Juan Nepomuceno Cipriano de la Santissima Trinidad painted under his mother's name—Picasso.

• • • • • •

An electric eel will short-circuit itself if it is put into salt water.

• • • • • •

Baboons cannot throw overhand.

• • • • • •

The face of comic book hero Captain Marvel was modeled after Fred MacMurray.

• • • • • •

English writer Ben Johnson was buried standing up in Westminster Abbey because he couldn't afford normal grave space.

• • • • • •

A spider has transparent blood.

• • • • • •

"I", the first person singular, is capitalized in English—the only language to do so.

• • • • • •

Octavio Guillen and Adriana Martinez were married in Mexico City in 1969 after a world record engagement of 67 years.

• • • • • •

*Oh, Susanna* earned composer Stephen Collins Foster the grand sum of fifty dollars.

• • • • • •

Eye Spy Dept.—Sherlock Holmes writer Arthur Conan Doyle was an opthalmologist.

• • • • • •

The state flower of Alaska is, appropriately, the forget-me-not.

• • • • • •

C.W. Post introduced coupons in 1895 when he offered "one-cent off" to kick off sales for his new cereal, Post's Grape Nuts.

• • • • • •

Annie Oakley's nickname was *Little Sure Shot.*

• • • • • •

A college mathematician has calculated that we spend five years of our lives waiting for things: waiting on lines, on telephones, in traffic, and so on.

• • • • • •

There were no significant historical accomplishments during the Millard Fillmore administration. He did, however, negotiate a deal with Peru over the use of guano—bird droppings.

• • • • • •

## Bathroom Trivia

No one knows who wrote the bathtub nursery rhyme *Rub a Dub Dub.*

• • • • • •

A duck frequently swims while sleeping.

• • • • • •

The Suez Canal was originally slated to be the site for the Statue of Liberty.

## Trivia Test

What did the 1940 Tokyo Olympic Games and the 1944 London Olympic Games have in common?

*They were both cancelled.*

Western Europe is sinking at the rate of one inch every ten years.

• • • • • •

The Statue of Liberty's pedestal was more expensive than Lady Liberty herself.

• • • • • •

"Gymnasium" stems from the Greek word *gymnos* which means "naked". And that's how the ancient Greek athletes practiced—in the raw.

• • • • • •

You might have guessed that the most widespread disease in the world is tooth decay.

• • • • • •

According to an old English time unit, one moment is 1 ½ minutes.

• • • • • •

The average office chair on wheels travels about eight miles per year.

• • • • • •

Calvin Coolidge was sworn in as U.S. President by his father.

• • • • • •

Because she wrote for up to 14 hours a day, *Little Women* author Louisa May Alcott alternated writing with her right and left hand to avoid writer's cramp.

• • • • • •

A cow spends an average of 18 hours a day chewing.

• • • • • •

Andy Johnson was a tailor who made his own clothes—until he became President of the United States.

• • • • • •

How fast is "in a jiffy"? Faster than you can say it. A "jiffy" is equal to one one-hundred-thousand-billion-billionths of a second, according to lexicographers.

• • • • • •

More women are millionaires than men in the U.S.

• • • • • •

Only one fifth of the Sahara Desert is sand. The rest of the world's largest desert is barren rock and rubble.

• • • • • •

More monuments have been built to honor Buddha than anyone else.

• • • • • •

It takes about four pounds of potatoes to make a pound of potato chips.

• • • • • •

Vincent van Gogh didn't begin to draw until he was 27.

• • • • • •

Sauerkraut originated in China some 1,000 years before it became a favorite in Germany.

• • • • • •

A pigeon's feathers weigh more than its bones.

• • • • • •

One-third of all the canned fish in the U.S. is eaten by cats.

• • • • • •

Your lungs use about 12,500 quarts of air each day.

• • • • • •

Wildlife lover John J. Audubon was also a wildlife killer. He shot as many as one hundred birds a day, using the victims as models for his paintings.

• • • • • •

The inside of a cucumber is 20 degrees (F) cooler than the air temperature on a warm summer day.

• • • • • •

A.C. Gilbert was a United States pole vaulter in the 1908 Olympics. A year later he was scaling new heights with his invention of the Erecter Set.

• • • • • •

## Bathroom Trivia

More than two million residents of Mexico City have no running water in their homes.

• • • • • •

"E" is the most commonly used letter in the English language, but not in Ernest Vincent Wright's book. The author wrote a 50,000 word novel, *Gadsby*, without using the letter at all.

• • • • • •

0 degrees longitude, 0 degrees latitude is in the Atlantic Ocean.

• • • • • •

In baseball. a left-handed pitcher is a *southpaw*. This term comes from the fact that most baseball diamonds are laid out with home plate toward the west so the sun won't bother the batter. The left-handed hurler, consequently, faces the west with his pitching arm to the south.

• • • • • •

---

## Trivia Test

What was the last name of Virginia, the eight year old who wrote to the *New York Sun* and asked if there really was a Santa Claus?

*O'Hanlon*

---

*Turn On*, a television series hosted by Tim Conway, proved to be a turn off. It premiered on February 5, 1969 and was cancelled the same day.

• • • • • •

Franklin Delano Roosevelt always kept a gun under his pillow while he was president.

• • • • • •

Aluminum was spelled "aluminium" until 1925 in the U.S.

• • • • • •

### Bathroom Trivia

Balneology is the science of the therapeutic use of bathing.

• • • • • •

# The Sporting Quiz

1. According to regulations, a race horse's name can be no longer than how many letters?

2. In the *Mutt & Jeff* comic strip, who was Jeff named after?

3. What three sports can one win by going backwards?

4. What is baseball great Tom Seaver's first name?

5. The score of a forfeited baseball game is 9-0. What is the score of a forfeited softball game?

6. Name the sport that began in India and was originally called "poona".

7. Two men who have nothing to do with baseball are in the Hall of Fame in Cooperstown, N.Y. Who are they?

8. In a record-setting performance, this man used a six iron and drove a golf ball some 400 yards. Who was it and on what course did he achieve this feat?

9. There's no disguising that Frederick Winthrop Thayer came up with this sporting invention in 1878. What is it?

10. Can you name the doctor who was on the U.S. rowing team in the 1924 Olympic Games in Paris?

11. "Small bowls" was a popular game among the likes of George Washington, Thomas Jefferson and John Adams. By what name do we know "small bowls" today?

12. Match these balls with the maximum weight allowed in each of their respective sports:

    A. basketball      1. 16 oz.
    B. soccer         2. 9.88 oz.
    C. baseball       3. 22.9 oz.
    D. football        4. 15 oz.
    E. volleyball      5. 5.25 oz.

13. Vinko Bogataj is seen each week on a popular network TV program. Who is he?

14. What soap opera star played big league baseball for the Cleveland Indians?

15. A horse named Broker's Tip won only one race in its entire career. What was it?

# Answers—The Sporting Quiz

1. *18 letters.*
2. *Boxer Jim Jeffries.*
3. *Rowing, the backstroke, and tug of war.*
4. *George.*
5. *7-0.*
6. *Badminton.*
7. *Abbott and Costello, for their "Who's On First?" routine.*
8. *Alan Shepard, on the moon.*
9. *Catcher's mask.*
10. *Benjamin Spock.*
11. *Marbles.*
12. *A-3, B-1, C-5, D-4, E-2.*
13. *The skier shown crashing off the ski jump in the introduction of ABC's "Wide World of Sports".*
14. *John Berardino (Dr. Steven Hardy on "General Hospital").*
15. *The Kentucky Derby in 1933.*

Thomas Edison preferred Braille to visual reading.

• • • • • •

Comedian Alan King made a record 83 appearances on *The Ed Sullivan Show.*

• • • • • •

The owl is no smarter than other birds. It may have been given its "wise" image because of its scholarly looks.

• • • • • •

There are 100 tiles, 98 letter and 2 blank, in the game of Scrabble.

• • • • • •

Winston Churchill believed that petting black cats brought him good luck.

• • • • • •

Birds have no sweat glands.

• • • • • •

Four out of five people who try out a new pen will write their own name.

• • • • • •

The state of Washington was going to be called Columbia until one legislator claimed it would always be confused with the District of Columbia. And so it became Washington.

• • • • • •

The lens in your eye grows throughout your life.

• • • • • •

A snail mates only once in its lifetime. And when it does, it mates in typical snail fashion, taking half a day to do it.

• • • • • •

True or False? Mark Twain was born in Florida.
That's true. Florida was a small community in Missouri. Twain then grew up in nearby Hannibal.

• • • • • •

The singular of the word scampi, as in shrimp, is scampo.

• • • • • •

A baseball catcher squats an average of 16 times an inning, not counting warmups.

• • • • • •

The name of the Camel cigarettes camel is *Old Joe*.

• • • • • •

The reason beer steins had lids was to keep flies out.

• • • • • •

Silent Cal Coolidge was just that as far as the telephone was concerned. The former president refused to use it.

---

## Trivia Test

Dr. Bunting's Remedy became more popularly known as what product?

*Noxzema.*

---

All polar bears are lefties.

• • • • • •

The original Stanley Cup, a silver bowl given to the National Hockey League champion each year, was worth $48.67 when Lord Stanley of Preston donated it back in 1893.

• • • • • •

The pound cake's name comes from the pound of butter used to make it.

• • • • • •

An undertaker was called "Doctor" during the Civil War.

• • • • • •

They say that glass gets stronger the longer it stays under water, the only known substance to do so.

• • • • • •

The shortest word in the English language which has all the vowels, including "y", is *facetiously*.

• • • • • •

We throw rice at weddings, but the Romans threw wheat.

• • • • • •

Until Thomas Edison suggested using "Hello", most people answered their phones by saying "Ahoy".

• • • • • •

A ping pong ball weighs 2.2399 to 2.6761 grams.

• • • • • •

If the headwind is greater than a plane's maximum speed, the aircraft will fly backwards.

• • • • • •

Dog sleds delivered mail in Alaska as late as 1963.

• • • • • •

## Bathroom Trivia

In 1879, a Proctor and Gamble employee operating a soap-mixing machine forgot to turn it off during lunchtime. The mixture was beaten to a froth so light that the cakes of soap bobbed around in the kettle. The plant foreman turned the mistake into a big moneymaker. He figured floating soap just might be the icing on the cake—such was the serendipitous discovery of Ivory Soap.

• • • • • •

Writer Washington Irving gave New York City the nickname *Gotham* in his 1807 *Salmagundi Papers.*

• • • • • •

The ampersand - & - is the world's oldest known symbol and is common among hundreds of languages.

• • • • • •

Ho Ho Ho! Saint Nicholas is the patron saint of pawnbrokers.

• • • • • •

There are no penguins at the North Pole. They can only be found south of the equator.

• • • • • •

The average person sheds 40 pounds of skin in a lifetime.

• • • • • •

There are 570 miles of shoreline in New York City.

• • • • • •

Montague and Capulet were better known by their first names—Romeo and Juliet.

• • • • • •

A baby whale is a "calf".

• • • • • •

The working title of the sizzling television serial *Dallas* was *Houston.*

• • • • • •

Cigarette Smokers—Warning: The world's largest airline may be dangerous to your health—or sanity. Aeroflot, Russia's national airline, allows smoking only after being airborne for four hours.

• • • • • •

A male lion can wolf down 75 pounds of meat at one meal.

• • • • • •

Of America's 2.3 billion acres of land, its original proprietors, native Indian tribes, now own 2 percent of it.

• • • • • •

There are 3,000 divorces a day in the U.S.

• • • • • •

George Washington, Thomas Jefferson and Alexander Hamilton were avid billiards players.

• • • • • •

The origin of "God bless you" is nothing to sneeze at. An old superstition had it that when someone sneezed, their soul momentarily left their body through the nostrils. This enabled the devil to creep in and prevent the return of the soul, but by saying "God bless you" the devil was stopped cold from entering the body.

• • • • • •

Telephone poles in Kenya and Uganda are higher than in other parts of the world because they have to allow for the height of giraffes.

• • • • • •

## Bathroom Trivia

It has been said that during the entire time Michelangelo painted the Sistine Chapel—four years—he never bathed.

• • • • • •

Troy Donahue played Merle Johnson in the movie *The Godfather II*. Merle Johnson is Donahue's real name.

• • • • • •

Your fingernails grow about two inches a year.

• • • • • •

Cowboy Roy Rogers was born on November 5, 1912 at 412 Second Street in Cincinnati, Ohio. That site is now second base at Riverfront Stadium, home of the Cincinnati Reds.

• • • • • •

An adult moth never eats.

• • • • • •

*Straight and Narrow* are two intersecting streets in Paterson, New Jersey.

• • • • • •

Alexandre Dumas used blue paper to write his novels, yellow paper for his poetry, and white paper to write his magazine articles.

• • • • • •

No matter how low or high it flies, an airplane's shadow appears the same size.

• • • • • •

## Bathroom Trivia

Ancient Arabians who bathed regularly were tax exempt.

• • • • • •

There are more than twice as many radios as people in the U.S.

• • • • • •

Next time your foot falls asleep you'll know to call it *taresthesia.*

• • • • • •

A newborn panda is smaller than a mouse.

• • • • • •

In Hawaii they get you coming and going with the same word. *Aloha* means both "hello" and "goodbye".

• • • • • •

Heinz sells three hundred million bottles of ketchup a year, almost one and a half bottles for every person in the U.S.

• • • • • •

Most hummingbirds weigh less than a penny.

---

## Trivia Test

The December 21, 1928 front page headline of the *New York Times* read "Waldorf-Astoria Sold. Fifty-Story Building to be Erected." What building was that?

*The Empire State Building, which became 102 stories, not 50.*

Screened Out—Saudi Arabia's eight and a half million people have no movie theater to go to.

● ● ● ● ● ●

## Bathroom Trivia

Australian Arron Marshall holds the world record for the longest shower—336 hours from July 29 to August 12, 1978. There is no record on the world record for a water bill.

● ● ● ● ● ●

Abraham Lincoln didn't particularly care to see *Our American Cousin* on that fateful night of April 14, 1865. He had already seen the play.

● ● ● ● ● ●

The theme song of Mexican outlaw Pancho Villa, *La Cucaracha*, means "the cockroach".

● ● ● ● ● ●

The Academy Awards Oscar trophy weighs 8 lbs., 13 oz.

● ● ● ● ● ●

You'll find more brown M&M's than any other color in a package of that candy.

● ● ● ● ● ●

Herb Alpert named his son after the first two notes of the musical scale—*Dore*.

● ● ● ● ● ●

Cows can be identified by noseprints.

● ● ● ● ● ●

London's Buckingham Palace has 602 rooms.

● ● ● ● ● ●

England and Zanzibar fought the shortest war in history in 1896. The British were victorious in the battle that lasted 38 minutes.

• • • • • •

A quarter weighs one-fifth of an ounce.

• • • • • •

William Phelps Eno (1858-1945) originated stop signs, one-way streets and other roadway regulations to earn himself recognition as the "Father of Traffic Safety". Eno never learned to drive a car.

• • • • • •

Scientists say that sharks are ten times more likely to attack a man than a woman.

• • • • • •

---

## Trivia Test

Thomas Edison copyrighted the first motion picture in the U.S. on January 1, 1894. What was its title?

*Record of a Sneeze.*

---

Your hearing is not as sharp on a full stomach.

• • • • • •

The Atlantic Ocean widens about one centimeter a year.

• • • • • •

## Bathroom Trivia

Howard Hughes kept magazines and books in the bathroom where he scouted movie prospects. (He spent much time there, ailing from chronic constipation.)

• • • • • •

If you have just come down with a cold, the National Health Foundation says you should wait at least six days before kissing someone.

• • • • • •

Vichyssoise does not come from France. The thick potato soup was created at the Ritz-Carlton Hotel in New York by head chef Louis Diat.

• • • • • •

Your chances are 3 in 100,000 of living to be older than 100 in North America.

• • • • • •

A giraffe has a 17 inch tongue.

• • • • • •

Opera superstar Luciano Pavarotti keeps a bent nail in his pocket for good luck when he performs.

• • • • • •

John F. Kennedy was the only U.S. president survived by both his parents.

• • • • • •

They may have been called "water catchers", but the cuffs on men's pants were originally made to hold cigar ashes.

• • • • • •

Actress Sally Struthers was once the voice of "Pebbles" on *The Flintstones* cartoons.

• • • • • •

Ten million Tootsie Rolls are made every day.

• • • • • •

The American Society for the Study of Headaches says that four out of five migraine sufferers are women.

---

## Trivia Test

What three animals move their front and hind legs on one side and then their front and hind legs on the other side when they walk?

*A cat, camel and giraffe.*

---

During the Middle Ages, a barber was a doctor and dentist as well as a haircutter.

• • • • • •

The most frequently sung tune in the U.S. is *Happy Birthday to You.*

• • • • • •

The main ingredient for both bricks and plate-glass windows is sand.

• • • • • •

They live an average of 77 years and have the longest life span in the United States—nuns.

• • • • • •

A bee's buzzing sound comes from the rapid up and down movement of its wings.

• • • • • •

President Theodore Roosevelt was a notoriously loud snorer.

• • • • • •

In 1779, four years after his historic midnight ride, Paul Revere was brought up on charges of "unsoldierly behavior tending towards cowardice". Revere was cleared, but an added irony to the development was the fact that the grandson of the general who made the accusation against Revere was Henry Wadsworth Longfellow, author of *Midnight Ride of Paul Revere*.

• • • • • •

An elephant's heart weighs about 45 lbs.

• • • • • •

## Bathroom Trivia

Every day Americans flush 6.8 billion gallons of water down their toilets.

• • • • • •

We call it the "French kiss" but in the French tongue it's called the "English kiss".

• • • • • •

Andrew Johnson is the only president to later become a senator.

• • • • • •

There are 2,598,960 possible hands in a five-card poker game.

• • • • • •

Alfred Nobel invented dynamite. Lesser known is that he was also the pioneer of plywood.

• • • • • •

Thomas Jefferson played the fiddle.

* * * * * *

Because of a reflex action, a rattlesnake can bite you up to a half hour after it's dead.

* * * * * *

Hunters killed 948 deer in Connecticut in 1978. Automobile drivers killed more than a thousand.

* * * * * *

A wink takes one tenth of a second.

---

## Trivia Test

What two five-letter words end with the letter "y" and do not contain the vowels a, e, i, o or u?

*Pygmy and gypsy.*

---

The Leaning Tower of Pisa bends an extra 1.25 millimeters every year and is expected to topple over somewhere between the year 2010 and 2020.

* * * * * *

The average person will catch 140 colds in a lifetime.

* * * * * *

Rube Goldberg, famed for his cartoons of crazy inventions, was a sewer engineer for the city of San Francisco.

* * * * * *

A camel hair brush is made of squirrel fur.

• • • • • •

The planet Saturn, like some others, is made up primarily of liquids or gasses and is less dense than water. If you placed it in a bathtub—a very big bathtub—it would float.

• • • • • •

If you have at least 5/8 of a torn dollar bill, it can be redeemed at full value.

• • • • • •

Botanically speaking, the onion is a lily.

• • • • • •

When a living thing is in a state of suspended animation during the winter, it's known as hibernation. But what's it called during the summer? —*Estivation.*

• • • • • •

## Bathroom Trivia

In 1851 Benjamin T. Babbitt became the first manufacturer to put soap bars in a wrapper. Up till then, soap was made in loaves which the grocer sliced and then weighed, much the same as cheese.

• • • • • •

What's Up Doc? ... 15 percent of Americans claim they've never had a headache ... Less than 50 percent catch a cold during the course of a year ... One-third of Americans have high blood pressure ... The average person gets sick 2.19 times a year and is bedridden for 6 days... The National Institute of Mental Health reports that 15 percent of the folks who visit doctors think they're sick but are really suffering from hypochondria ... 50 percent of the visits to the school nurse are made by 15 percent of the students.

• • • • • •

# Last Call

Aviation pioneer Orville Wright died of natural causes on January 30, 1948. The same day, ironically, there were three plane crashes which killed some 50 people in the U.S.

The last guillotine execution on record occurred May 12, 1973 in France.

F. Scott Fitzgerald was reading Princeton University's alumni magazine when he died.

*Suttee* was an ancient Hindu ritual in which a widow cremated herself over her husband's pyre.

Poet John Keats was only twenty-six when he died.

Juan Carlos, King of Spain, accidentally shot and killed his brother with an air-rifle when he was a boy.

Actor Lionel Barrymore was reading *Macbeth* aloud when he died.

# Famous Last Words

"Whose house is this? What street are we in? Why did you bring me here?"
>—*William Cullen Bryant, poet (1794-1878).*

"Oh, God, here I go!"
>—*Max Baer, World Heavyweight Boxing Champion (1909-1959).*

"l must go in, for the fog is rising."
>—*Emily Dickinson, poet (1830-1886).*

"Adios, compadre!"
>—*Kit Carson, U.S. frontiersman (1809-1868).*

"I still live—poetry."
        —*Daniel Webster, American statesman (1782-1852).*

"My head, my head!"
        —*Robert Louis Stevenson, Scottish novelist (1850-1894).*

"Amen."
                —*Brigham Young, Mormon leader (1801-1877).*

# The Bathroom Library

THE BATHROOM BASKETBALL BOOK
THE BATHROOM GUEST BOOK
THE BATHROOM CROSSWORD PUZZLE BOOK
THE BATHROOM DIGEST
THE BATHROOM TRIVIA BOOK
THE BATHROOM ENTERTAINMENT BOOK
THE BATHROOM SPORTS QUIZ BOOK
THE BATHROOM SPORTS QUOTE BOOK
THE BATHROOM GAME BOOK
THE BATHROOM BASEBALL BOOK
THE BATHROOM FOOTBALL BOOK
THE BATHROOM GOLF BOOK
THE BATHROOM INSPIRATION BOOK
THE BATHROOM TRIVIA BOOK - Volume II
THE BATHROOM ROCK 'N ROLL BOOK
THE BATHROOM JOKE BOOK

For further information, write to:
Red-Letter Press, Inc.
P.O. Box 393
Saddle River, N.J. 07458